KRISSY BALLINGER

make & play

NATURAL DIY RECIPES FOR KIDS

contents

54

35

107

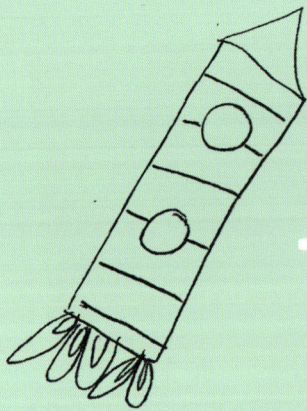

a message for the future warriors of the world

Hi! I'm so very glad you're reading this page because it is where I get to tell you a little bit about me and my favourite little people (my kids), and exactly why I created this book for the future grown-ups of the world – that's you!

So, my name is Krissy (my parents call me Kristina, but that's all a bit too formal, don't you think?). I am a mum to Charlotte (she's 11) and Lucas (he's almost 9). I know every mum thinks their kids are the coolest, but these two really are the coolest. They love making stuff and playing with stuff and you could only imagine how excited they were when I said I was going to write a book for kids and that they would be my chief recipe-testers!

Back to me: I have a lovely husband (his name is Rod) and we live in Perth, Australia, where it is almost always sunny, and windy! I used to be a school teacher and taught health and physical education. Now I write lots of fun and natural recipes for people like you (and the grown-ups too).

Health and wellness are very important to me and my family. We have certain rules in our house to make sure that we stay as healthy and happy as possible.

This means:

We eat good, nutritious, real food, almost all of the time (don't worry, we still have treats!).

We don't use sprays, powders, creams and liquids that have nasties in them. This means we get in the kitchen and make our own things like washing powder and sunscreen (cool hey?).

We get outside and exercise in fresh air and sunlight every single day. Moving is good for your body, good for your brain, and way less boring than hanging out indoors all the time!

We try to always think happy thoughts. Positive thoughts = positive energy, and when we're bouncing around with happiness, life is way more fun.

You know what else is really, really, super-duper important to us? Planet earth, is what!

It is so important that we start taking care of this place that we all call home, after all, we only get one of them. Sometimes people are a little disrespectful in the way they treat our planet, from littering to pollution, to wasteful activities. I think, and many people agree with me (including the person who gave you this book, probably), that earth needs your help. I'm going to help you understand why …

You won't be a child forever. You will grow up. You have a lot of time on earth. I'm calling on you to make the grown-ups listen now, so they can help to get the planet to a happy place – are you up to the job? If so, keep reading …

Tell them you want to simplify things, buy less stuff and throw less away, recycle more, use less nasties by making more of your own stuff for your body and your home. Make them listen (it might help to bat those eyelids, pout a little and be cute, so they won't be able to resist!). Good luck, beautiful future-warriors.

When I wrote the recipes for this book, I did my best to make sure they were all:

Fun for kids, of course!

As natural, kid- and earth-friendly as possible.

Simple to make (either on your own depending on your age, or with just a little help from a grown-up).

I think, according to my chief recipe-testers, that I've ticked all those boxes. And I do hope, with all of my heart and soul, that you'll love every one of my recipes, and that you'll tell your friends how much fun it is to make your own face paint, goop and bath bombs so that more and more people are having as much natural fun as you (and me)!

5

information for the grown-ups

Thank you for picking up this book, and for investing time and effort into making natural and fun stuff with the little people in your life. I can guarantee that they're going to have so much fun making these recipes, as will you (I hope)!

Before the kids get started, there are a few important considerations:

★ I've written this book for kids, and the language I use throughout will speak to them, inspire and motivate them, and keep them busy for hours, creating and playing.

★ Read all of the introduction information (pages 9-27) before starting, especially if DIY is a relatively new concept for you. It's good to get some grounding information on safety and shelf life, ingredients, colouring options, storage etc.

★ Depending on the age and ability of the kids, some may be able to make most of the recipes by themselves, and others will need a little (or a lot of) help. There is a guide on each recipe as to how much help they might need, but you'll need to be the judge of that, of course.

★ Make sure the kids don't taste any of the ingredients or completed recipes. While they're designed to be non-toxic, they're not intended to be consumed. Please supervise small children around ingredients, tools and small objects.

★ Refer to the information on page 26 if you have any questions regarding the symbols on each recipe. Once you see what each of them means, they will be easy to understand.

The most important message I have for you, however, is this:

Our children are our future leaders, our future earth-inhabitants. We want them to grow up safe, happy and healthy. We want them to realise their dreams, to perhaps have thriving families of their own someday. It's not hard to see that the world we live in is in a state of disarray, with attitudes swinging heavily towards convenience and speed over longevity and sustainability. Something needs to change, and it needs to change quickly.

I ask you to think about your words, attitude and actions around children. Reduce, reuse and recycle, buy less but buy better, learn to read labels and consider making your own products for home and body (I have you covered in this space, look for my book Naturally Inspired, Simple DIY Recipes for Body Care and Cleaning). Slow down, talk about things, stay positive. No one is perfect (whatever that even means), but aim for 80/20 – do what you know is right, as often as you can (80%), and go easy on yourself for the rest of the time (20%).

Stress is rarely a good feeling, and children are so intuitive, so be mindful of your attitude and behaviour as they're endlessly 'picking up what you're putting down'.

I've kept this book as simple as possible, and tried to keep the ingredients lists to a bare minimum. You should be able to get away with a handful of staple ingredients that will get you through a number of recipes.

Enjoy all that this book has to offer.

My favourte recipe
Is the Foaming sludge.
I like it because it puffs up.
I hope that you like the
recipes in my mums
book.
Lucas

This book has a lot
of fun activities for
you to do, and at
the same time you're
being nice to the planet
Hope you love it as
much as I do.
♡ Charlotte

safety first, always!

Just like cooking, you should always be careful when making fun, natural do-it-yourself recipes.

Here are a few things you will need to read and understand:

⚡ Always get permission from the grown-up in charge to make these recipes. Always, always, always. No exceptions. Okay? Good!

⚡ Be especially careful when you're using things like knives, glass bowls, blenders, ovens and stovetops. They're hot, they're sharp and they command caution and respect!

⚡ Just because we're using natural ingredients, doesn't mean that they shouldn't be treated with respect. That means, be careful not to get them in your eyes, nose and mouth.

⚡ Take care not to inhale any powdered ingredients, even if that means wearing a mask or asking a grown-up to do those bits for you.

⚡ Make sure you're not sensitive to, or irritated by, any of the ingredients in my recipes before touching or using them. That might mean you need to do a little spot test on a small area of skin – ask a grown-up to help with this. Sometimes gloves are useful too.

⚡ If you decide to make any of these recipes and give them to friends (they'll make the best party favours and birthday presents, trust me!), make sure you also give them a list of every ingredient used – just in case they're allergic to anything.

⚡ Sometimes people are irritated by essential oils, especially kids, so I haven't used them very often in my recipes. If you don't have any, or the grown-ups don't want you to use them, just leave them out.

⚡ Floors and benches get so slippery when you're working with butters and oils so make sure you move around slowly and carefully, and keep things super clean and organised.

⚡ Be careful when using body scrubs, salts, bath bombs etc. in the bath and shower as they may leave the tub and floor a little slippery.

the ingredients you'll be using

Let me tell you a little bit about the ingredients you'll need to make the recipes in this book.

Most will sound familiar; some will sound strange. Those that you can't find in the pantry can usually be sourced from health food stores, bulk food stores, specialty online retailers and sometimes supermarkets.

While I encourage you to experiment and swap ingredients, please keep in mind that I have written and tested all of my recipes using the ingredients listed. If you decide to swap ingredients or leave them out, your results might be different to mine. And you know what, there is no harm in trying, you might even like your results better than mine – winning!

MOSTLY COMMON, PANTRY INGREDIENTS

Agar agar powder is a natural thickening and gelling ingredient that comes from red algae.

Arrowroot flour is a very fine, gluten-free flour. It can be swapped for cornflour but the recipes may turn out a little different.

Bicarb soda is technically called sodium bicarbonate, but is also known as bicarb or baking soda. It is mainly used in this book to give some recipes a sizzle and fizz.

Brown sugar is a soft and gentle sugar, great for gently scrubbing skin. It also gives some DIY recipes a lovely texture.

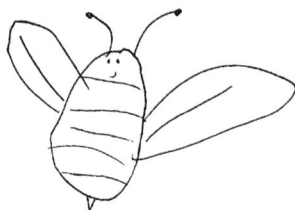

Chia seeds are actually awesome for you to eat. They also absorb a lot of water and become jelly-ish, which is very handy in the Stretchy Spotty Sticky Goop recipe (page 98).

Citric acid is mainly used in this book to give some recipes a sizzle and fizz. It also acts as a preservative and helps to make things last a little longer.

Clear alcohol is used to remove bubbles on top of melt and pour soap that was just poured. Vodka is a popular choice (just make sure you have adult supervision).

Cocoa powder is made from roasted cacao beans, and smells chocolaty. You can also use cacao powder.

Coconut oil is good to eat and good for your skin. It is hard when it's cold and runny when it's warm.

Fine salt is a very common household ingredient and often used as a preservative in DIY recipes.

Gelatin powder comes from animals (look for an ethical brand that is natural and unflavoured) and helps to make the Wobbly Jelly Soap (page 65), ummm, wobbly! I haven't found an effective substitute for this.

Himalayan salt is so rich in amazing minerals that our bodies need and love. You can pretty much swap and use any salt you like in any of my recipes.

Honey comes from bees, is deliciously sticky and is great for skin.

Olive oil is a very common and versatile household oil. It can be swapped out for any other liquid oil.

Plain flour is a common baking flour.

Psyllium husk is the outer coating of the psyllium seed. When boiled in the Rubber Flubber recipe (page 100), it becomes slimy, thick and stretchy.

Rice is not only good for eating! It can be milled down to a fine powder which has a gritty, slippery feel and is also a gentle way to scrub skin.

Self-raising flour is a common baking flour but with added ingredients to make it rise.

Spices like cinnamon sticks, cloves and star anise look great in the Friendly Fragrance recipe (page 49).

Turmeric powder is used to add colour, or a little aroma.

Vanilla bean paste helps to make the Good Enough to Eat Face Scrub (page 35) smell good enough to eat!

Vinegar is used in the Garden Stew (page 117) to create a fizzy delight!

Water should always be purified, or boiled and cooled. This will help to make your DIY last longer.

White sugar is a little rougher on the skin than brown sugar.

FRESH FOODS

Citrus zest is the outside (rind) of citrus fruits like lemon, lime, orange and grapefruit. It adds a delightful aroma to your DIY.

Strawberries are a fun and fruity ingredient to use in natural scrubs.

Yoghurt – even though I suggest plain, you can use any flavour.

ESSENTIAL OILS
see page 13

more on next page

OTHER DIY INGREDIENTS

Activated charcoal is a very fine, black powder. I prefer to use charcoal that has been made from natural sources, like coconut shells.

Aloe vera gel can often have sneaky ingredients in it, so beware. Using the juicy bit from fresh aloe vera plants isn't a good idea in the Melting Putty (page 110) because it won't last long.

Beeswax pellets help to make DIY balms and butters solid. Find beeswax that is filtered, so that all the little bits have been removed. Pellets are easy to measure and melt, but you can use beeswax blocks, just be careful grating it.

Epsom salt is a wonderful, soothing ingredient to add to DIY body care recipes, especially those that you use in the bath.

Liquid castile soap is a natural soap that is usually made from coconuts and/or olives.

Magnesium chloride flakes are an awesome way to boost your energy levels, plus you'll sleep better too.

Melt and pour soap base is kind of like the cheat's way to make soap. It can be easily melted, have things added to it, and then set in a supercool mould. Make sure your soap base doesn't have any nasty fragrance or preservatives.

Shea butter is a white/off-white, tacky butter, full of nourishing goodness for your skin. If you swap shea butter for cocoa or mango butter, your recipes will turn out firmer.

Soap (bar) I am talking about a regular bar of soap. Just be sure to find one without fragrance and other icky ingredients.

Vegetable glycerine comes from plants like coconut, soy and palm, and draws moisture towards it, which helps to prevent the Face-Friendly Paint (page 79) from cracking.

White clay is chalky (perfect for chalk!), but also gives the paint recipes a creamy texture. If you swap for another clay, the recipe outcome may be different.

Zinc oxide powder is a natural way to reflect the sun's harmful UV rays from the body. Always use non-nano particles and be very careful not to inhale this powder (wear a mask, or ask a grown-up for help).

GARDEN

These are fairly obvious, hey?

Dirt, flowers and buds, seeds, grass, herbs, leaves, sand, stones, twigs

TREASURES

I'm thinking little toys, or pretty collectables. Just make sure they are clean and small enough to use in the recipe you're making.

Figurines, toy dinosaurs, fairies, mini erasers, shells

COLOURING

see page 14

essential oils

Essential oils are concentrated, natural oils from plants, and they are a lovely way to make things smell beautiful. Of course, they also have other benefits, but for the purposes of this book, they're used for their super-smelly powers. I'm not a fan of fake smells (artificial fragrance) like perfume, air fresheners, smelly stickers and erasers because I don't think they are very good for our bodies. They actually give me headaches and make my belly feel a little icky. Have you ever noticed that happen to you? Our bodies are very clever, and they like to give us warning signals when they feel 'danger'. I think that fake smells should be avoided.

When I want something to smell lovely, I use beautiful plant-based essential oils!

I actually don't use essential oils that often in this book, but you can definitely add some wherever you like (or leave them out altogether). Just check with the grown-ups in charge, and keep in mind that not all essential oils are suitable for everyone, so extra research might be needed. Also, make sure you're using 100% pure essential oils, and avoid anything that is labelled as a fragrance oil.

Here is a list of some common essential oils that are generally safe for kids to use, when diluted appropriately:

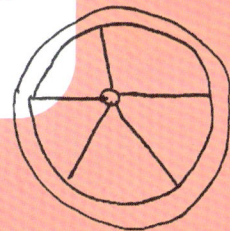

BERGAMOT ♥ GERANIUM ✶ GRAPEFRUIT

LAVENDER ✶ LEMON ♥ LIME ✶ MANDARIN

ORANGE ♥ ROSE ✶ SPEARMINT

TANGERINE ♥ TEA TREE

colour, colour, colour!

Colour is exciting, colour is inviting, colour is fun - don't you agree?

I love colour, so do my kids, but we've learned over time to appreciate the softer shades that natural colours give us.

But that doesn't mean that you can't use brighter colours; it can be way more fun to have colours that pop, for sure.

Sometimes, many colours that are available for us to use in cooking and DIY aren't actually that great for people or the planet. Some of them are made from petroleum, some are made from insects (gross but true!) and some are sourced by disregarding the rights of other humans. In our home, when we DIY, we mostly avoid micas and artificial food colouring, but I'd love to encourage you and your grown-ups to source the best possible colours that you can, and to use the ones that meet your needs.

WHICH COLOURINGS SHOULD YOU USE IN THESE RECIPES?

Well, whichever you like (most of the time!). On each recipe page, I will usually just list 'colouring' as an ingredient. It is up to you how much colouring you use, and whether you choose natural or artificial, in each recipe; it really depends on how bright you want the colour to be.

Sometimes, a specific colouring really is the better choice and, in these cases, I'll point out which one I think you should use by saying: **colouring (must be powder)**, for example. Feel free to have a play around though; you are most welcome to experiment, in fact, I encourage it. Just keep in mind that some natural powdered colours and spices don't mix perfectly well into oils and waxes, and in some recipes, liquids just aren't a good choice.

A NOTE ON CHOOSING COLOURING

The aim of this book is to create excitement about natural DIY and to get you having fun.

You will hopefully even be able to stop buying some products from the shops and make them yourself. While I like for everything to be as natural as possible, in our house we love the **80/20 rule**; basically we try to do the absolute, very best we can 80% of the time, and we give ourselves 20% grace for those things we can't control or that we choose to take shortcuts with. This makes a natural life much more doable, fun and relaxing!

Here is an example: if you only have regular, artificial food colouring in your cupboard, and you want to turn your Stretchy Spotty Sticky Goop (page 98) green, then I think you should use it. Be proud and focus on the fact that you're doing such a great job of making natural goodies. Also, with my recipes, you won't be eating the final products, so you and the grown-ups might not be as worried about the colouring you use.

Who thinks this is a good rule to follow?

MAKING YOUR OWN COLOURING

You can dehydrate (dry) and blitz, or boil down, many fruits and vegetables to get natural colourings. Although these types of colourings can work in natural DIY, from my experience, the liquids just don't last very long, the powders are often too lumpy and gritty, and I think they are best left for colouring icing, cakes and other food-based recipes.

Here are some of my favourite, and easy-to-find, natural powdered colourings.

Yellow/orange
turmeric, paprika, pumpkin, ginger

Green
green spirulina, kale, spinach

Red
tomato, paprika

Blue
blue spirulina

Black/brown
activated charcoal, cocoa, cinnamon, coffee

Pink/purple
beetroot, pitaya (dragon fruit), hibiscus

There are many brands on the market that are selling natural liquid colours too.

COLOUR COMPARISON

I coloured some Fun Dough (page 105) to show you the difference between:

1. cosmetic micas
2. natural powdered colouring
3. artificial liquid colouring

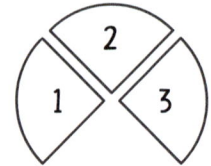

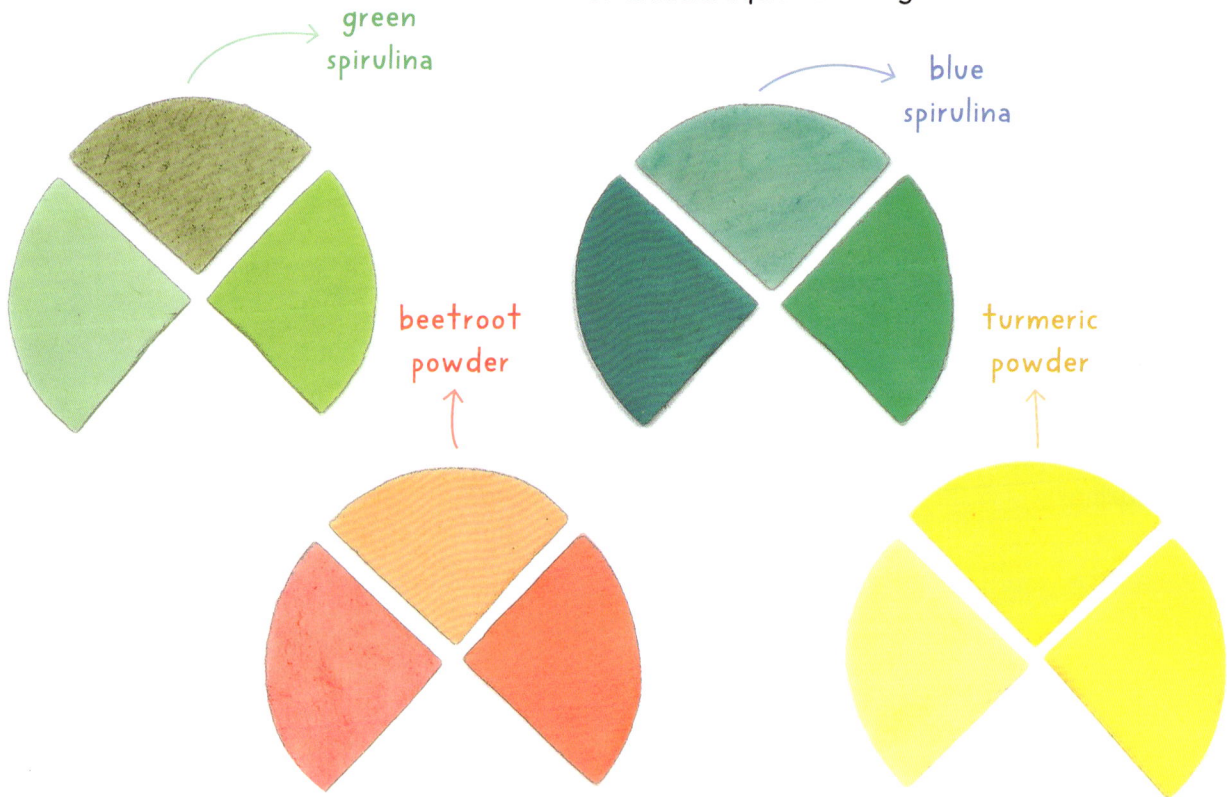

green spirulina

blue spirulina

beetroot powder

turmeric powder

THE MAIN TYPES OF COLOURING

Natural (liquid and powder) – typically made from fruits and vegetables, and sometimes you need to use quite a lot to get a good punch of colour.

Artificial (liquid and powder) – typically used in cooking and cake-decorating, usually very bright, and you may not need very much to get a big result.

Cosmetic micas – minerals naturally formed from rocks and used to add shimmer and colour to recipes. Many are coated in bright, artificial colours. Always handle these with caution, never inhale them (wearing a mask, or asking a grown-up for help, is a good idea) and make sure you're using cosmetic-grade micas that are designed to be used on the body.

'It's good for the environment and helps stop landfill, plus it's fun and good for you.'

LILY (10)

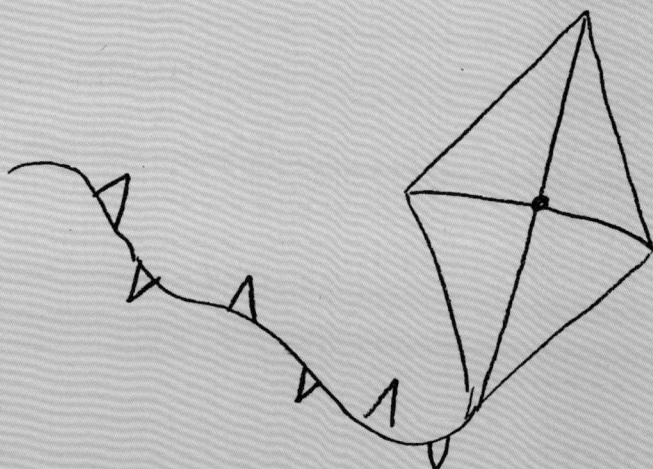

essential tools and equipment

Here is a list of the tools and equipment you'll need to make the recipes in this book.

See, natural DIY is just about as straightforward as making a cake in your kitchen! The containers and moulds might sound a little strange initially, but the photo on the next page should give you a better idea.

- ☐ Baking paper
- ☐ Baking tray
- ☐ Blender
- ☐ Bucket
- ☐ Chopping board
- ☐ Citrus zester
- ☐ Cookie cutters
- ☐ Dish
- ☐ Egg carton
- ☐ Fork
- ☐ Fridge/freezer
- ☐ Funnel
- ☐ Glass jug with an open handle (small and medium)

- ☐ Hole punch
- ☐ Ice cube tray
- ☐ Kettle
- ☐ Knife
- ☐ Measuring cups
- ☐ Measuring spoons
- ☐ Metal straw
- ☐ Microwave (optional)
- ☐ Mixing bowls
- ☐ Mixing spoons
- ☐ Oven
- ☐ Oven mitt or tea towel
- ☐ Paddle-pop/ icy pole stick

- ☐ Paintbrushes
- ☐ Plate
- ☐ Rolling pin
- ☐ Saucepans
- ☐ Scales (digital)
- ☐ Spatula (flexible silicone)
- ☐ Stovetop
- ☐ Timer
- ☐ Tray
- ☐ Whisk

CONTAINERS AND MOULDS (VARYING SIZES)

- ☐ Lip balm tubes or pots
- ☐ Containers, with lids
- ☐ Twist tube/push-up containers
- ☐ Squeeze-style containers
- ☐ Clear glass roller-type bottles
- ☐ Moulds (flexible silicone, metal/hard plastic)

looking after your DIY goodies

You will notice symbols on each of my recipes (see page 26) which aim to give you a rough idea of how long your goodies will last once they have been made, and whether they can be stored at room temperature or whether they need to go in the fridge. Of course, I can't be too specific with shelf life because I don't know exactly how you're making and storing your goodies.

There are plenty of things you should (and shouldn't) do to make sure your goodies last as long as possible, and reduce the number of germs that might want to invade your recipes.

♥ Sometimes the things we make can turn 'bad' before we can see any evidence with our naked eyes or smell it with our noses! Always be sensible. If you (or the grown-ups) think something looks or smells funny, and you're in doubt, it's best to chuck it out.

♥ While I'd be very excited to hear that you're making goodies to share with friends and family, just be aware that these recipes are not designed to be mass-produced and sold at markets and fetes; the idea is to make enough for yourself (and maybe a little extra to share) to use within a reasonable period of time.

♥ Always use clean hands, equipment and surfaces when making and playing.

♥ Water can be a breeding ground for germs, so make sure you're always using purified or boiled and cooled water.

choosing containers & storage tips

★ When choosing containers, unless I give you a specific type and size, choose one with a lid that is airtight, and that your goodies will comfortably fit into.

★ Even though I prefer to use glass at home, you might find plastic is the safest option when storing your recipes.

★ Make sure that the containers you're using to make and store your goodies are clean – washing in warm/hot (naturally) soapy water is usually enough to do the trick, but sterilising is even better.

★ I like to rinse any bottles that have narrow openings with a little clear alcohol before filling – the higher the proof the better, but ask a grown-up to do this bit for you.

★ It is best to store your goodies in a cool and dry place, away from sunlight, dust and damp air. Keep water (and moisture) from contaminating your finished products.

cleaning up

My best piece of advice here is to keep things as tidy and organised as possible while you're DIY-ing. Not only does this make it much easier to clean up at the end, but it means there is less chance of you getting muddled up, or losing the equipment you need.

Most recipes are very simple to clean up after. You'll just need to scrape out as much as you can (a flexible silicone spatula is very handy) and then wash up in a sink of warm (naturally) soapy water.

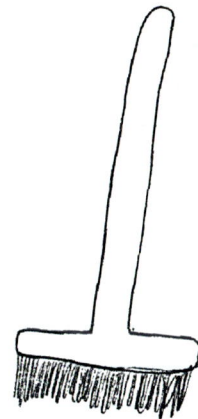

When you're cleaning up after making recipes like Lip Balm (page 33) or Moisturising Bars (page 44), then you'll need to follow these steps:

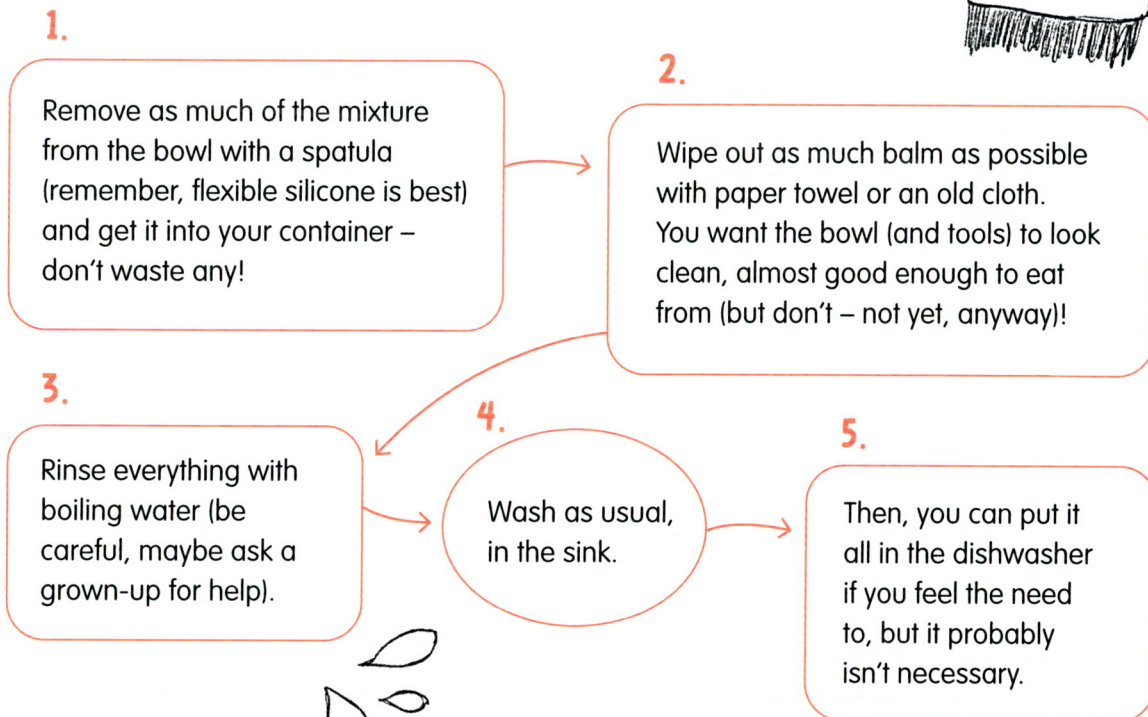

1.
Remove as much of the mixture from the bowl with a spatula (remember, flexible silicone is best) and get it into your container – don't waste any!

2.
Wipe out as much balm as possible with paper towel or an old cloth. You want the bowl (and tools) to look clean, almost good enough to eat from (but don't – not yet, anyway)!

3.
Rinse everything with boiling water (be careful, maybe ask a grown-up for help).

4.
Wash as usual, in the sink.

5.
Then, you can put it all in the dishwasher if you feel the need to, but it probably isn't necessary.

handy tips for recipe success!

WEIGHING AND MEASURING INGREDIENTS

You will notice that I use scales to weigh just about everything in my recipes. I use metric measurements (if you're after imperial measurements, there is a conversion chart for you on page 122). This just makes things much easier than using measuring jugs, cups and spoons. So, get yourself a set of simple digital scales that measure to the gram.

Always place your bowl or jug on the scales and 'tare' them (this means resetting your scales to read '0') between each ingredient added.

When a small amount of an ingredient is needed, or it isn't required to be too precise, I will use a teaspoon or tablespoon to measure (I have used Australian measuring spoons). When using measuring spoons, make sure your spoon is level with the brim, not heaped or overflowing.

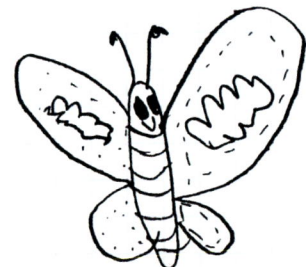

MIXING

A wooden spoon will do the job well. A good technique to use when mixing, especially flour and oil, is to gently press down, and rotate your mixing spoon – this squashes the ingredients together and helps to combine them.

Carefully mix in a way that means your ingredients aren't puffing up and exploding out of the bowl – we don't want to be breathing any of those ingredients into our lungs, regardless of how natural they are (remember you can wear a mask, or ask a grown-up for help).

TRANSFERRING AND DIVIDING MIXTURES

If I ask you to divide a mixture evenly between containers, you can measure precisely with measuring spoons or scales, or simply guess. Make sure you get as much of the mixture out of your mixing bowl and into the containers or moulds – don't waste any! A very handy way to do this is to use a flexible silicone spatula.

85

RESTING TIME

Some recipes need time to rest or set before you can use them. Sometimes I will ask you to pop balms into the fridge to set, which helps to keep them from going grainy over time. Some goodies just need time to rest on your kitchen bench – don't be tempted to poke and play with them before they're ready!

melting (and heating) techniques

DOUBLE BOILER METHOD

I use a double boiler because it allows for even and gentle melting of ingredients, and just about everyone already has one at home. All you need is a glass jug with an open handle, a saucepan and a stovetop. Here's what you need to do:

⚡ Add the ingredients to the glass jug.

⚡ Fill the saucepan with enough water to cover the bottom (a few centimetres deep) and pop your glass jug in the saucepan, so the handle is hooked over the side.

⚡ Place the saucepan on the stovetop, set the heat to moderate, and get the water simmering. **Make sure your saucepan doesn't run out of water!**

⚡ Stir every now and again, with a mixing spoon – this will help your ingredients to melt faster. **Be careful of steam from the saucepan!**

⚡ Once the ingredients are fully melted, switch off the heat.

⚡ Carefully remove the glass jug from the saucepan and place it on your work surface. **Pop a tea towel or wooden chopping board down to protect it from heat.**

You might like to use a tea towel or oven mitt – OUCH!

Of course, there is always more than one way to get the job done, and you might like to use a microwave or thermal appliance for some, or all, of the steps. In most cases you can, but keep in mind that my recipes were written and perfected while I used the methods listed, so if you change the way you do it, the results might also change.

THERMAL APPLIANCE METHOD

For recipes that require melting, mixing and/or kneading, a thermal appliance can sometimes get the job done faster. Here are a few tips for converting a traditional recipe method into a thermal appliance method:

⚡ While ingredients can be weighed straight into the bowl, I prefer separate digital scales, as they are the most precise, especially for small quantities. You can pop the thermal appliance bowl on the kitchen scales and weigh in the ingredients that way.

⚡ When melting, keep the temperature between 60-70 ℃ and on low speed.

⚡ When it comes to basic mixing, I recommend low to moderate speed.

⚡ Blitzing and milling will need to be done at the highest speed.

⚡ Most thermal appliances have a special function (or attachment) that will come in handy when kneading.

⚡ Be sure to use the little cup on the lid of your thermal appliance when mixing and milling to prevent the ingredients from escaping.

MICROWAVE METHOD

If you choose to use a microwave, just keep your zapping to short 15-20 second bursts, on the lowest power setting. Check and mix the ingredients each time.

And please, don't stand too close!

what do the symbols mean?

CAUTION

Stovetops are hot, knives are sharp, blenders are loud!

When you see this symbol on any recipe, it's a warning that you'll be using equipment that you need to be super careful with, or that you might need extra help from a grown-up.

STORING

Most recipes are fine to be stored at room temperature, but some need to be kept in the fridge.

can be stored at room temperature

should be kept in the fridge

★ Remember to always read the entire recipe before starting!

LEVEL

Kids of different ages have different levels of skill. This section aims to give you a bit of an idea of how tricky a recipe is.

pretty simple and straightforward instructions

usually has extra steps, might be a little tricky for some

fiddly recipe, usually lots of steps, help from a grown-up may be needed

TIME

This will give you a rough idea of how long the recipe will take to make, from the start to the end. Of course this depends on your age and ability. If the recipe needs extra setting or drying time before you can use it, I'll tell you.

usually between 10-20 minutes

approximately 20-30 minutes

will take 30 minutes or more

SHELF LIFE

This is a guide as to how long your goodies should last. Go back to page 20 for more information.

use it right away

you've got a day or two

should keep for a week or so

good for a few weeks

you should get 4 weeks +

get set for success

Before you start any recipe or activity, ask yourself the following questions:

☐ Do I have permission from a grown-up (or is one able to watch and help me)?

☐ Have I read through the important safety information on page 9?

☐ Is my workspace clean and clear of clutter?

☐ Is my workspace surface sensitive to heat?

☐ Have I read the recipe from the top to toe?

☐ Do I have enough time to finish the recipe?

☐ Do I have all of the tools and the ingredients out on my workspace?

☐ Am I excited and ready to make something natural and fun?

Check with a grown-up - if the recipe involves the stovetop or the oven, you might need to pop something down to protect your work surface, like a chopping board, mat or towel.

This is an absolute must.

No one likes a rush job!

This is absolutely essential!

If you can say YES to all of the above, then you're ready to go!

let's get making!

happy honey lip polish

MAKES
80 g

WHAT YOU NEED

50 g rice
brown or white

25 g coconut oil
make sure it's runny

1 tsp honey

TOOLS

blender

scales

small mixing bowl

measuring spoon

mixing spoon

container with lid

LET'S GET MAKING

1. Grab the blender jug and weigh in the rice.

2. Blend until it is fine (like powder), then empty it into the mixing bowl.

3. Now weigh in the coconut oil and measure in the honey, and mix well.

4. Transfer the lip polish into the container.

TIME TO PLAY

Gently massage a small amount of the polish mixture over wet lips and rinse well with water.

★ You could also give your hands, feet and body a polish with this recipe.

On a cold day, you may need to scoop a little polish out and soften it between your fingers before using it.

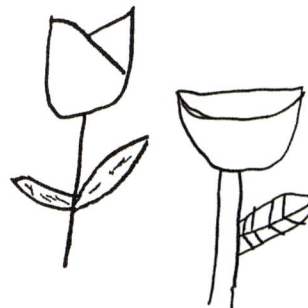

LEVEL

TIME

SHELF LIFE

STORE

choc mint lip balm

MAKES
6

WHAT YOU NEED

25 g shea butter

25 g olive oil

10 g beeswax pellets

1/2 tsp cocoa powder

5 drops of spearmint
essential oil
see page 13

TOOLS

small glass jug

scales

double boiler
head back to page 24
for helpful info

mixing spoon

measuring spoon

lip balm tubes or pots
x6; 10 g capacity

fridge

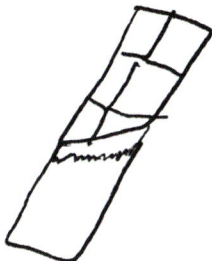

LET'S GET MAKING

1. Grab the glass jug and weigh in the shea butter,
   olive oil and beeswax pellets.

2. Use the double boiler to melt the ingredients.
   Stir gently every now and again.

3. Now measure in the cocoa powder and add the
   spearmint essential oil, and stir well.

4. Carefully pour the mixture into the lip balm tubes or
   pots and pop them into the fridge until they are set
   – this will take around 30 minutes.

TIME TO PLAY

Smooth balm over lips as often as you feel the
need (which will probably be every 7-8 minutes,
and that's okay!).

Be quick when
pouring, the mixture
sets very quickly!

These make an
awesome party
favour or gift idea.

LEVEL

TIME

+ setting time

**SHELF
LIFE**

STORE

33

good enough to eat face scrub

MAKES enough for one use

WHAT YOU NEED

1 tsp brown sugar

1/2 tsp white sugar

1/2 tsp honey

1/2 tsp olive oil

1/2 tsp plain yoghurt

a dash of vanilla bean paste

TOOLS

measuring spoon(s)

small mixing bowl

mixing spoon

LET'S GET MAKING

Measure all of the ingredients into the mixing bowl and mix well.

TIME TO PLAY

Wet your face and gently massage a small amount of the scrub mixture all over (be sure to avoid your eyes). Then, rinse well with water.

LEVEL

TIME

SHELF LIFE

Why not double or triple this recipe and get your family to try it, or make it at your next sleepover party!

choc mud face mask

MAKES
enough for one use

LEVEL

TIME

SHELF LIFE

WHAT YOU NEED

1 tsp plain yoghurt

1 tsp cocoa powder

1 tsp honey

TOOLS

measuring spoon

small mixing bowl

mixing spoon

LET'S GET MAKING

Measure all of the ingredients into the mixing bowl and mix well.

TIME TO PLAY

Using your fingers, spread the mixture all over your face (be sure to avoid your eyes). Relax while you leave it on for 10-15 minutes, before rinsing well with water.

Chocolate

'This recipe is so delicious, you might want to lick your fingers clean once you're done!'

mess-around make-up

LEVEL

TIME

SHELF LIFE

STORE

WHAT YOU NEED

50 g olive oil

5 g beeswax pellets

30 g arrowroot flour

colouring
x5; micas work best;
see pages 14-16

TOOLS

small glass jug

scales

double boiler
head back to page 24
for helpful info

mixing spoon

containers with lids
x5; 30 g capacity

measuring spoon

LET'S GET MAKING

1. Grab the glass jug and weigh in the olive oil and beeswax pellets.

2. Use the double boiler to melt the ingredients. Stir gently every now and again.

3. Now weigh in the arrowroot flour and stir well so that there are no lumpy bits.

4. Divide the mixture evenly between the containers and add a different colouring (for best results, use at least 1 teaspoon of mica) to each one, then mix carefully.

5. Your make-up is ready to use, no need to wait for it to set!

TIME TO PLAY

Using a clean make-up brush, apply to your eyelids, lips or cheeks.

Be very careful not to inhale the loose mica dust. A face mask to cover your mouth and nose is a good idea (or ask a grown-up for help).

Want my *bestest* ever tip to remove make-up? It's olive oil! Simply massage a small amount all over your face and then wipe off with a warm/hot, wet face washer.

sizzle & soak

MAKES
enough for
one use

LEVEL

TIME

SHELF LIFE

WHAT YOU NEED

1 lemon
zest only

50 g bicarb soda

50 g epsom salt

40 g citric acid

10 g arrowroot flour

1/4 tsp turmeric powder

TOOLS

citrus zester

small mixing bowl

scales

measuring spoon

mixing spoon

LET'S GET MAKING

1. Use the zester to carefully remove the zest from the lemon, straight into the mixing bowl.

2. Now weigh in the bicarb soda, epsom salt, citric acid and arrowroot flour.

3. Measure in the turmeric powder and mix well.

TIME TO PLAY

Fill a basin or bucket with warm water and add the mixture. It'll be fun and fizzy. Soak your feet for 10-15 minutes. You might like to moisturise with a little olive oil when you're done (then, pop some socks on so you don't slip).

If you want to gift this soak or save it for another time, use dried lemon zest.

41

♥ This one smells amazing, but don't eat it!

berry scrub

MAKES enough for one use

WHAT YOU NEED

1 strawberry
small; ripe; no leaves

2 tbsp sugar
any sugar will do

1 tbsp epsom salt

1 tsp honey

TOOLS

small mixing bowl

fork

measuring spoon(s)

LET'S GET MAKING

1. Pop the strawberry into the mixing bowl and mash it with a fork, until it's nice and mushy.

2. Measure in the sugar, epsom salt and honey, and mix well.

TIME TO PLAY

Hop in the shower and gently massage the scrub mixture all over your skin. Then, rinse well with water.

LEVEL

TIME

SHELF LIFE

doughnut moisturising body bars

MAKES 2

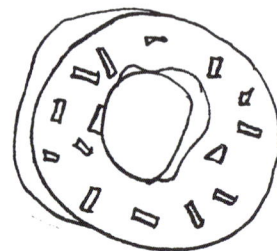

LEVEL

TIME
+ setting time

SHELF LIFE

STORE

WHAT YOU NEED

50 g shea butter

50 g olive oil

25 g beeswax pellets

colouring
x2; micas work best;
see pages 14-16

5-10 drops of essential oils
optional; see page 13

TOOLS

small glass jug

scales

double boiler
head back to page 24
for helpful info

mixing spoon

small dish

doughnut-shaped
flexible moulds
x2; 50 g capacity

fridge

container with lid

LET'S GET MAKING

1st part – colourful swirls and splatters

1. Grab the glass jug and weigh in the shea butter, olive oil and beeswax pellets.

2. Use the double boiler to melt the ingredients. Stir gently every now and again.

3. Pour about 1 tablespoon of the melted mixture into the small dish and add the first lot of colouring, and mix well.

   ★ Pop the glass jug back in the saucepan so the mixture doesn't start to set.

4. Gently drizzle, or splatter, the mixture over the moulds to make the 'topping'. Be quick – it sets fast! You will have some left over, but using any less for this step will set too fast.

2nd part – main batch

5. Back to the glass jug: add the second lot of colouring, and the essential oils (if you're using them) and mix well.

6. Carefully fill the moulds with the mixture and place them into the fridge until they are set – this will take up to an hour.

7. Remove your body bars from their moulds and transfer them into the container.

If the mixture sets before you've finished with the splatters, pop the dish in a shallow bowl of hot water until it melts again.

TIME TO PLAY

Run a bar over your skin. Because your body is warm, it will gently melt. Massage the balm into your skin.

WHAT IS THE BEST PART ABOUT
MAKING YOUR OWN NATURAL GOODIES?

'We get to make
natural mess.'

VIOLET (7)

friendly fragrance

WHAT YOU NEED

dried bits and bobs
herbs, spices,
flower buds, petals,
citrus zest etc.

5-10 drops of
essential oils
see page 13

olive oil
enough to fill the
roller bottle

TOOLS

roller-type bottle(s)
clear; glass

small funnel
make sure it fits
into the opening of
the roller bottle(s)

LET'S GET MAKING

1. Grab a roller bottle and pop the little roller top off.

2. Fill it with some of the bits and bobs, about 1/3 full, then add the essential oils.

3. Now pop the funnel into the opening of the roller bottle and fill it, just short of the top, with olive oil.

4. Put the roller top and lid back on, and give it a little shake.

TIME TO PLAY

Roll the fragrance onto your skin as often as you like.

LEVEL

TIME

SHELF
LIFE

STORE

colour explosion bath bombs

MAKES 2

LEVEL

TIME

+ drying time

SHELF LIFE

STORE

WHAT YOU NEED

150 g bicarb soda

70 g citric acid
make sure it's super fine

30 g epsom salt
make sure it's super fine

20 g arrowroot flour

20 g olive oil

5-10 drops of essential oils
optional; see page 13

colouring
must be powder;
see pages 14-16

TOOLS

large mixing bowl

scales

mixing spoon

small mixing bowl

flexible moulds x2;
25 g capacity; any shape

plate

sphere-shaped
metal/hard plastic mould
6 cm diameter

container with lid

LET'S GET MAKING

1st part – mini bath bombs

1. Grab the large mixing bowl and weigh in the bicarb soda, citric acid, epsom salt, arrowroot flour and olive oil.

2. Add the essential oils (if you're using them) and mix very, very well.

3. To test the mixture, squeeze a little in your hands. If it only just holds together, it's good to go. If it is very crumbly, add an extra 1/2 teaspoon of olive oil and keep mixing (don't be tempted to add too much oil, trust me!).

   ★ If your bath bombs don't hold together, it could be because your mixture isn't fully combined. Mixing in a blender should solve that issue.

4. Now grab the small mixing bowl and weigh in 50 g of the mixture, and the colouring, and mix well. ⚡

5. Fill the flexible moulds with the mixture, pressing down firmly. Brush any extra mixture back into the small mixing bowl.

6. Wait a few minutes before carefully removing the bath bombs from their moulds, then place them on the plate to dry. (If your bath bombs crumble, just empty and try again.)

   ★ Do not disturb them while they are resting - bath bombs are fussy little things!

50

2nd part – finishing the bath bombs

7. Back to the main batch of mixture in the large mixing bowl: grab one half of the sphere-shaped mould and fill it 3/4 full with mixture. Press down but don't pack it in too tightly.

8. Gently place a mini bath bomb in the centre and add more mixture around the sides, gently pressing down to pack the mixture in. Set this aside.

9. Fill the second half of the large mould until full (press down but don't pack it in too tightly).

10. Sprinkle a little mixture around, and over the top of, both halves so the mixture looks like it is loosely overflowing.

11. Join the moulds together and squash down firmly (don't twist). There will be extra mixture that spills out – just wipe this away and back into the large mixing bowl.

12. Remove the bath bomb by gently prying the moulds apart (sometimes a little tap with a spoon helps).

★ If your bath bomb doesn't work, go back to step 7.

13. Pop the bath bomb on the plate to dry. Remember not to disturb it while it is resting.

14. Repeat steps 7-13 one more time, so you have 2 large bath bombs.

15. Leave your bath bombs for at least 24 hours to dry (in a cool, dry place) before transferring them into the container.

TIME TO PLAY

Drop a bath bomb into the bath and watch in awe as it fizzes madly, and then changes colour, like magic!

♥ Sprinkle the leftover mixture into your next bath.

⚡ The more colour you use, the brighter the explosion but beware, micas can make a mess if you use too much.

Because this recipe uses oil and colours, it could make your tub tricky to clean - you might like to help the grown-ups clean up when you're done.

photos on next page 51

Charlotte loves making these bath bombs. These pictures might help you get a better idea of this fiddly (but seriously fun) recipe!

step 10.

step 8.

step 11.

funny face bath bombs

MAKES depends!

LEVEL

TIME
+ drying time

SHELF LIFE

STORE

WHAT YOU NEED

150 g bicarb soda

70 g citric acid
make sure it's super fine

30 g epsom salt
make sure it's super fine

20 g arrowroot flour

20 g olive oil

colouring
optional; must be
powder; see pages 14-16

5-10 drops of
essential oils
optional; see page 13

bath bomb paint

TOOLS

large mixing bowl

scales

mixing spoon

flexible moulds
any size or shape

plate

thin paintbrush

container with lid

BATH BOMB PAINT

Simply grab a small dish and add **1 teaspoon of colouring** (micas for colour, and activated charcoal or cocoa powder for black/brown) and **enough olive oil** to make a thin, runny paste, and mix well. Be careful, charcoal is very messy so don't use too much paint, especially if you're using black.

EXTRA IDEA!

Hide a little treasure inside your bath bombs for a fun surprise at bath time. Small objects like figurines, toy dinosaurs, fairies, mini erasers and shells are just a few cool ideas.

LET'S GET MAKING

1. Grab the mixing bowl and weigh in the bicarb soda, citric acid, epsom salt, arrowroot flour, and olive oil.

2. Add the colouring and essential oils (if you're using them), and mix very, very well.

3. To test the mixture, squeeze a little in your hands. If it only just holds together, it's good to go. If it is very crumbly, add an extra 1/2 teaspoon of olive oil and keep mixing (don't be tempted to add too much oil, trust me!).

   ★ If your bath bombs don't hold together, it could be because your mixture isn't fully combined. Mixing in a blender should solve that issue.

4. Fill each mould with the mixture, pressing down firmly. Brush any extra mixture back into the mixing bowl.

5. Wait a few minutes before carefully removing the bath bombs from their moulds, then place them on the plate to dry. (If your bath bombs crumble, just empty and try again.)

   ★ Do not disturb them while they are resting - bath bombs are fussy little things!

6. Leave your bath bombs for at least 24 hours to dry (in a cool, dry place). Once they're dry, they'll be easier to paint.

7. To paint, make the Bath Bomb Paint and get creative. You can use my ideas as a guide or create something super cool.

8. Once you've finished painting, pop your bath bombs into the container.

TIME TO PLAY

Drop a bath bomb into the bath and watch it sizzle and fizz!

   ♥ Sprinkle the leftover mixture into your next bath.

Because this recipe uses oil and colours, it could make your tub tricky to clean - you might like to help the grown-ups clean up when you're done.

55

how will you save the world today?

- ☐ Take a reusable cup with you next time you get a takeaway juice
- ☐ Say no to plastic straws and shopping bags
- ☐ Pick up 3 pieces of litter in your street
- ☐ Walk or cycle, rather than drive, if possible
- ☐ Swap the kitchen bin liner for a few sheets of newspaper
- ☐ Smile at a stranger

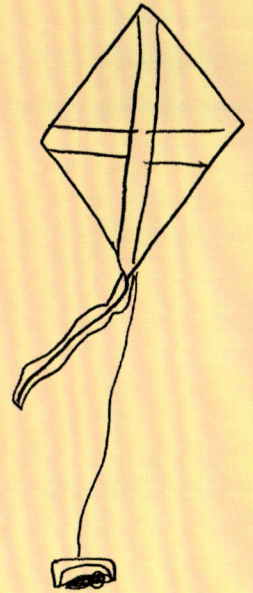

Need to relax after a busy day of playing? Try some Relaxing Bath Salts.

Throw 1 cup of magnesium chloride flakes into the bath for a big energy boost! You could also use ingredients like epsom salt, sea salt and himalayan salt – they're all known to help your busy body relax and restore.

fizzing bath dust

MAKES 300 g

WHAT YOU NEED

100 g bicarb soda

70 g citric acid

70 g epsom salt

40 g fine himalayan salt

20 g arrowroot flour

colouring
optional; must be powder;
see pages 14-16

5-10 drops of essential oils
optional; see page 13

TOOLS

large mixing bowl

scales

mixing spoon

tray

container with lid

LET'S GET MAKING

1. Grab the mixing bowl and weigh in the bicarb soda, citric acid, epsom salt, himalayan salt and arrowroot flour.

2. Add the colouring and essential oils (if you're using them), and mix well.

3. Spread the mixture onto the tray and leave it to dry for a day or so (in a cool, dry place), then crumble the mixture with your fingers.

4. Transfer your bath dust into the container.

TIME TO PLAY

Fill a bath with water and sprinkle a handful of the dust in and watch it fizz!

You may need to break the mixture up with a spoon if it sets a little in your container.

LEVEL

TIME

+ drying time

SHELF LIFE

STORE

watermelon sugar scrub cubes

LEVEL

TIME

SHELF LIFE

STORE

WHAT YOU NEED

200 g bar of soap
the most natural one you can find; chopped into small pieces (grape-size)

60 g olive oil

60 g shea butter

180 g white sugar

10-15 drops of essential oils
optional; see page 13

colouring
x2; green and pink/red; see pages 14-16

bath bomb paint
black; see page 54

TOOLS

blender

scales

medium glass jug

double boiler
head back to page 24 for helpful info

mixing spoon

small mixing bowl

measuring spoon

square container
approx. 15 x 15 x 5 cm

freezer

chopping board

knife

thin paintbrush

container with lid

'These make my skin feel so nice and soft!'

If your container has no 'flex', line it with some baking paper.

1st part – green layer

1. Grab the blender jug and weigh in the soap.

2. Blitz until it is fine and powdery, then transfer it into the glass jug.

3. Now weigh in the olive oil and shea butter.

4. Use the double boiler to melt the ingredients. Stir gently every now and again until the ingredients start to warm and soften (they won't melt).

5. Now weigh in the white sugar, and add the essential oils (if you're using them), and mix well.

6. Grab the small mixing bowl, and add about 4 (heaped) tablespoons of the mixture to it.

7. Colour this batch with the green colouring and mix well.

8. Add this mixture to your container and spread it out evenly, to cover the bottom. Press down firmly.

9. Pop the container in the freezer for 5 minutes.

2nd part – white layer

10. Take your container out of the freezer and spread about 2 (heaped) tablespoons of the (uncoloured) mixture evenly over the green layer. Press down firmly.

11. Pop the container back in the freezer for 5 minutes.

3rd part – pink layer

12. Colour the remaining mixture, in the glass jug, with pink/red colouring.

13. Spread this mixture evenly over the white layer, pressing down firmly, then smooth down the top as much as you can.

14. Pop the container into the freezer for 15-20 minutes (or until it feels solid to touch) before gently removing the slab of sugar scrub onto the chopping board.

15. Use the knife to carefully slice the watermelon slab into 9 even squares.

16. Using the Bath Bomb Paint, paint small 'seeds' randomly over the pink/red layer, then transfer your sugar cubes into the container.

TIME TO PLAY

Massage the bar over wet skin while you're in the bath or shower, and rinse well. Pop it on a soap dish between uses.

When spreading the mixture in the container, if you find it to be too messy, wait until it cools a little. Using wet fingers may also help.

photo on next page 61

'It's way more fun
to make your bath
stuff than going
to the boring shops
and buying it.'

HOLLY (6)

wobbly jelly soap

MAKES
depends!

WHAT YOU NEED

100 g hot water

10 g gelatin powder

1/2 tsp fine salt

100 g liquid castile soap

colouring
see pages 14-16

10 drops of essential oils
optional; see page 13

TOOLS

kettle

medium glass jug

scales

measuring spoon

whisk

flexible moulds
small; any shape

fridge

container with lid

LET'S GET MAKING

1. Boil the kettle (make sure there is enough water inside).

2. Grab the glass jug and weigh in the hot water and gelatin powder, and measure in the salt.

3. Whisk until the gelatin powder has mostly dissolved.

4. Now weigh in the castile soap, and add the colouring, and essential oils (if you're using them). Whisk again.

5. Pour the mixture into the moulds and pop them in the fridge to set – this could take a few hours.

6. Once set, pop your jellies out of their moulds and transfer them into the container.

TIME TO PLAY

Take one of these jellies out of the fridge and with you into the bath or shower. Use them just as you would soap, rinsing well when you're done.

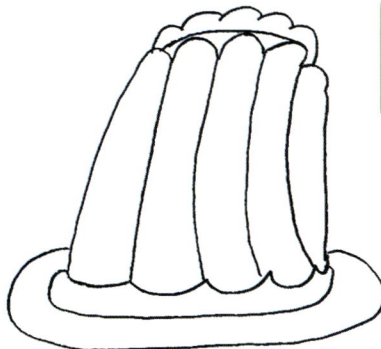

LEVEL

TIME

+ setting time

SHELF LIFE

STORE

Each jelly soap is designed to be used once.

soapy dough

MAKES 230 g

WHAT YOU NEED

130 g arrowroot flour
plus extra to dust your
work surface

100 g liquid castile soap

colouring
see pages 14-16

3-4 drops of essential oils
optional; see page 13

TOOLS

medium mixing bowl

scales

mixing spoon

container with lid

LET'S GET MAKING

1. Grab the mixing bowl and weigh in the arrowroot flour and castile soap.

2. Add in the colouring, and essential oils (if you're using them), and mix until the dough starts forming.

3. Dust your work surface with a little extra flour and pop the dough on top.

4. Knead until it is soft and stretchy, and no longer sticky. It should feel silky smooth, and easy to shape and mould.

5. Transfer your dough into the container.

TIME TO PLAY

You can either create dough shapes and let them set, then use these to wash yourself in the shower or bath – or take the dough to the tub with you to play and wash!

layered soapy icy poles

MAKES
1

LEVEL

TIME

+ setting time

SHELF LIFE

STORE

WHAT YOU NEED

90 g melt and pour soap base
clear or white; chopped into small pieces (grape-size)

colouring
x3; see pages 14–16

vegetable glycerine
a few drops; x3

15 drops of essential oils
optional; see page 13

1 tbsp clear alcohol
approx.; in a small spray bottle

TOOLS

small glass jug

scales

double boiler
head back to page 24 for helpful info

mixing spoon

small dish

icy pole-shaped mould
100 g capacity

spatula

paddle-pop/icy pole stick

container with lid

'I would totally have more fun using this soap in the shower.'

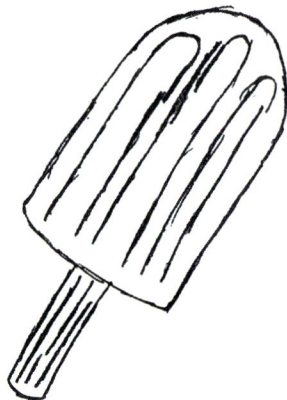

LET'S GET MAKING

1st part – first layer

1. Grab the glass jug and weigh in 30 g of the soap base.

2. Use the double boiler to melt the soap base. Stir gently every now and again.

   ★ While the soap base is melting, add one lot of colouring to the small dish with a few drops of vegetable glycerine and mix well.

3. Now add the colouring mixture and 5 drops of essential oils (if you're using them) to the melted soap base, and stir well.

4. Pour the soap carefully into the mould, keeping it off the sides (use the spatula to get as much mixture out as you can). It should only fill the mould to be 1/3 full.

5. Spray the top lightly with a little alcohol (this helps your soap to stick to the next layer, and gets rid of bubbles).

6. Leave your soap aside to set while you make the next layer.

   ★ You will only need to wash your jug before the next step if you have lots of coloured, soapy mess left behind, otherwise just carry on with a dirty jug.

2nd part – middle layer

7. Repeat steps 1-3, this time using a different colour.

8. Spray the first layer lightly with a little more alcohol, then pour the soap into the mould.

9. Give the soap another light spray with alcohol and set aside.

3rd part – final layer

10. Repeat steps 1-3, once again using a different colour.

11. Spray the middle layer lightly with a little more alcohol before you pour the final layer of soap.

12. Give the soap one last light spray with alcohol.

13. Carefully push a paddle-pop/icy pole stick in the centre of your soap until you feel it go through the middle layer and into the first layer.

14. Leave your soap to 'cure' for at least 24 hours, in a cool, dry place (don't put it in the fridge, or it'll sweat when you take it out).

15. Carefully remove your soapy icy pole from its mould (but don't yank the paddle-pop/icy pole stick too hard) and pop it into the container.

    ★ If your soap is difficult to remove from the mould, you can carefully dip it in some hot water for 10-20 seconds at a time, until you feel it loosening.

TIME TO PLAY

Use this soap just like you would use any other soap – these are just way more fun! Pop it on a soap dish between uses.

image on next page

69

buried treasure soap

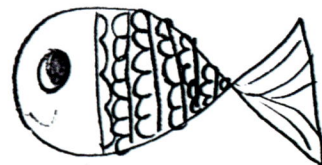

LEVEL

TIME

+ setting time

SHELF LIFE

STORE

WHAT YOU NEED

100 g melt and pour soap base
clear; chopped into small pieces (grape-size)

10-15 drops of essential oils
optional; see page 13

1 tbsp clear alcohol
approx.; in a small spray bottle

small treasure
figurine, toy dinosaur, fairy, mini eraser, shell etc.

TOOLS

small glass jug

scales

double boiler
head back to page 24 for helpful info

mixing spoon

flexible mould
100 g capacity

container with lid

LET'S GET MAKING

1. Grab the glass jug and weigh in the soap base.

2. Use the double boiler to melt the soap base. Stir gently every now and again.

3. Add in the essential oils (if you're using them) and stir well.

4. Carefully pour half of the soap into the mould and give the top a light spray with a little alcohol (this helps to get rid of any bubbles).

   ★ Pop the glass jug back in the saucepan so the soap doesn't start to set.

5. Wait for 5-10 minutes until a light 'crust' forms on the surface of the soap in the mould and place your treasure on top, pressing gently.

6. Now top up the mould carefully with the remaining soap and give it another light spray with a little alcohol.

   ★ If your treasure floats, just use a toothpick to gently push and press it down again.

7. Leave your soap to 'cure' for at least 24 hours, in a cool, dry place (don't put it in the fridge, or it'll sweat when you take it out).

8. Carefully remove your treasure soap from its mould and pop it into the container.

TIME TO PLAY

Use this soap just like you would use any other boring soap, and after each use, you'll get a little closer to the treasure on the inside! Pop it on a soap dish between uses.

colourful carnival zinc stick

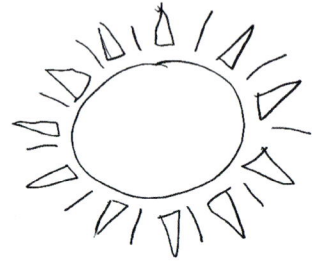

MAKES
1

LEVEL

TIME
+ setting time

SHELF LIFE

STORE

WHAT YOU NEED

40 g shea butter

20 g olive oil

5 g beeswax pellets

25 g zinc oxide powder
make sure it's
non-nano particles

colouring
must be powder;
see pages 14-16

TOOLS

small glass jug

scales

double boiler
head back to page 24
for helpful info

mixing spoon

twist tube/push-up
container
100 g capacity

fridge

You can leave out the colouring and have white zinc if you like.

LET'S GET MAKING

1. Grab the glass jug and weigh in the shea butter, olive oil and beeswax pellets.

2. Use the double boiler to melt the ingredients. Stir gently every now and again.

3. Now weigh in the zinc oxide powder and add the colouring. Stir, stir, stir.

4. Carefully pour the mixture into the container, and place it into the fridge until it is set – this may take up to an hour.

TIME TO PLAY

Apply the zinc to places that need a little extra protection from the sun, like your nose and cheeks (be sure to avoid your eyes). You might even like to wear it to your next school sports carnival.

Be *very* careful not to inhale zinc powder. A face mask to cover your mouth and nose is a good idea (or ask a grown-up for help).

inspiration for gift-giving

page
44

page
50

page
60

page
54

page
31

page
114

Thanks for being
The Best Teacher
Ever!

HAPPY
BIRTHDAY

page
81

page
33

page
49

face-friendly paint

WHAT YOU NEED

15 g white clay

15 g water

1 tsp vegetable glycerine

colouring
x3; see pages 14-16

TOOLS

small mixing bowl

scales

measuring spoon

mixing spoon

containers with lids
x3; 20 g capacity

LET'S GET MAKING

1. Grab the mixing bowl and weigh in the white clay and water.

2. Measure in the vegetable glycerine and mix until it is smooth and creamy.

3. Divide the mixture evenly between the containers and add a different colouring to each one, then mix well.

TIME TO PLAY

Paint your face as you like, just keep the paint thin so it doesn't crack too much as it sets (and be sure to avoid your eyes).

This washes off easily with water.

LEVEL

TIME

SHELF LIFE

STORE

79

paper paint

MAKES
3

WHAT YOU NEED

90 g hot water

15 g fine salt

60 g arrowroot flour

45 g white clay

colouring
x3; see pages 14-16

TOOLS

kettle

small mixing bowl

scales

mixing spoon

containers with lids
x3; 100 g capacity

LET'S GET MAKING

1. Boil the kettle (make sure there is enough water inside).

2. Grab the mixing bowl and weigh in the hot water and salt, and stir until the salt is mostly dissolved.

3. Now weigh in the arrowroot flour and white clay, and mix until the ingredients are smooth and creamy.

4. Divide the mixture evenly between the containers and add a different colouring to each one, then mix well.

TIME TO PLAY

Grab a piece of paper and paint away!

LEVEL

TIME

SHELF LIFE

STORE

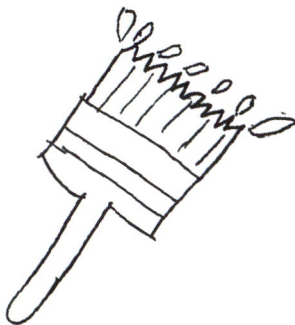

If your paint thickens up too much, just add a splash of water.

watercolour paint palette

MAKES
6

WHAT YOU NEED

80 g white clay

60 g water

colouring
x6; must be liquid;
see pages 14-16

TOOLS

small mixing bowl

scales

mixing spoon

egg carton
small; half-dozen

LET'S GET MAKING

1. Grab the mixing bowl and weigh in the white clay and water.

2. Mix really well, until the mixture is smooth, and there are no lumpy bits.

3. Divide the mixture evenly between the spaces in the egg carton and add a different colouring to each one, then mix well.

4. Let the paint dry for 3-4 days until it is hard.

TIME TO PLAY

Dip a paintbrush into water and massage over the paint until the colour 'melts'. Now you can paint your next masterpiece!

LEVEL

TIME

+ drying time

SHELF LIFE

STORE

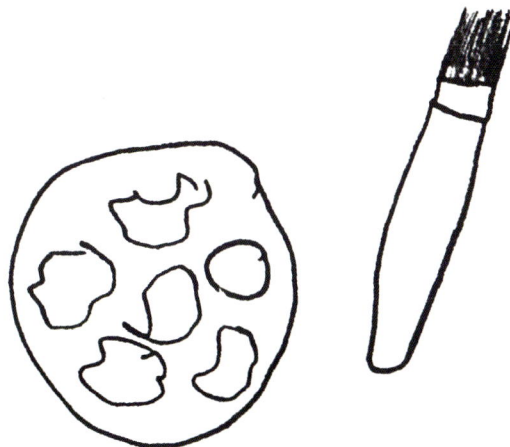

glossy sugar paint

WHAT YOU NEED

100 g water

40 g white sugar

1/2 tsp arrowroot flour

colouring
x3; must be liquid;
see pages 14-16

TOOLS

small saucepan

scales

measuring spoon

mixing spoon

stovetop

containers with lids
x3; 50 g capacity

LET'S GET MAKING

1. Grab the saucepan and weigh in the water and white sugar.

2. Measure in the arrowroot flour and mix well.

3. Place the saucepan on the stovetop, on moderate-high heat, and mix occasionally.

4. Bring the mixture to the boil for a count of 60 seconds, then switch off the heat.

5. Allow the mixture to cool down (for 5 minutes or so), before dividing it evenly between the containers.

6. Measure in a different colouring to each one, then mix well.

TIME TO PLAY

Paint away! Just keep the layers thin, or it will take a long time to dry.

LEVEL

TIME

SHELF LIFE

STORE

puffy paint

MAKES
5

WHAT YOU NEED

150 g water

150 g fine salt

80 g self-raising flour

40 g arrowroot flour

colouring
x5; see pages 14-16

TOOLS

medium mixing bowl

scales

mixing spoon

squeeze-style containers
x5; 100 g capacity

LET'S GET MAKING

1. Grab the mixing bowl and weigh in the water, salt, self-raising flour and arrowroot flour.

2. Mix really well, until the mixture is smooth and there are no lumps left.

3. Divide the mixture evenly between the containers and add a different colouring to each one, then shake well (or use a paddle-pop stick to jiggle and stir).

TIME TO PLAY

Squeeze different patterns onto paper, and then you have 3 choices:

★ Pop your paper in the microwave for 5-10 seconds (for the best puffy result).

★ Place your paper in the oven (200 °C) for 5 min (don't take your eyes off it!).

★ Let your paint air dry.

LEVEL

TIME

**SHELF
LIFE**

STORE

Over time, if the mixture thickens in the bottle, just add a little splash of water and shake well.

'They don't
harm your skin,
they're fun to
make and fun to
play with.'

ISLA (10)

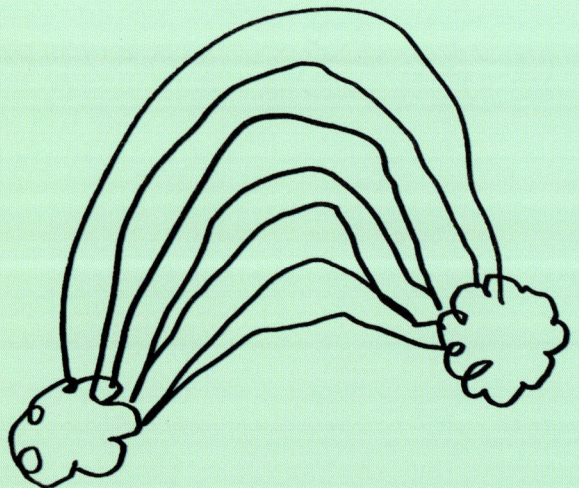

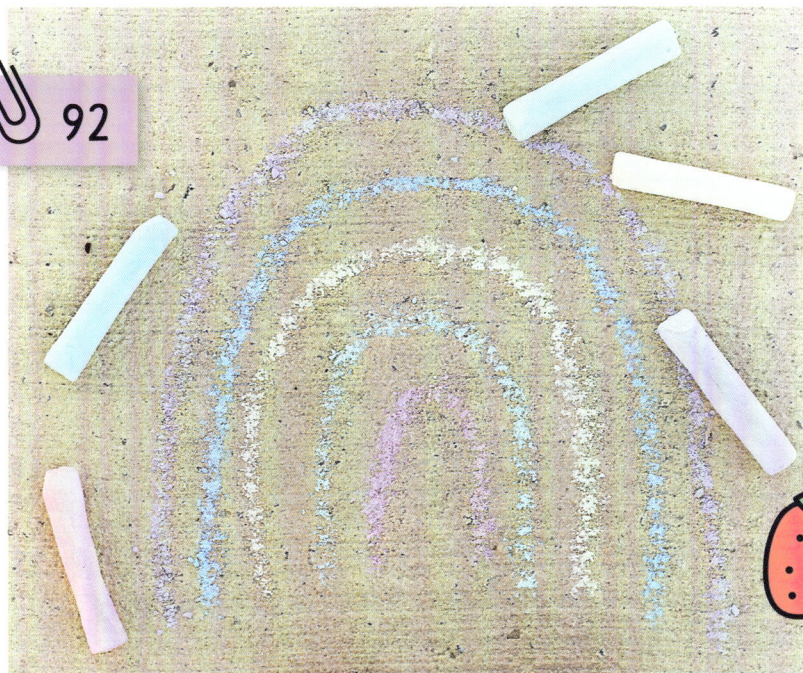

92

36

simple soapy crayons

MAKES 1

LEVEL

TIME
+ setting time

SHELF LIFE

STORE

WHAT YOU NEED

20 g melt and pour soap base
clear or white;
chopped into small pieces (grape-size)

colouring
must be liquid;
see pages 14-16

1 tbsp clear alcohol
approx.; in a small spray bottle

TOOLS

small glass jug

scales

double boiler
head back to page 24 for helpful info

mixing spoon

twist tube container
20 g capacity

LET'S GET MAKING

1. Grab the glass jug and weigh in the soap base.

2. Use the double boiler to melt the soap base. Stir gently every now and again.

3. Add the colouring and mix well.

4. Carefully pour the coloured soap into the twist tube container and give it a light spray with a little alcohol (this helps to get rid of any bubbles).

5. Leave your soapy crayon to set for at least 24 hours, in a cool, dry place (don't put it in the fridge, or it'll sweat when you take it out).

TIME TO PLAY

Use these like you would ordinary crayons (they can even be used in the bath tub – it washes off easily!).

If your crayon is not as strong in colour as you'd like, just carefully remove it from its container, gently melt again and add a little extra colour before pouring it back into the container.

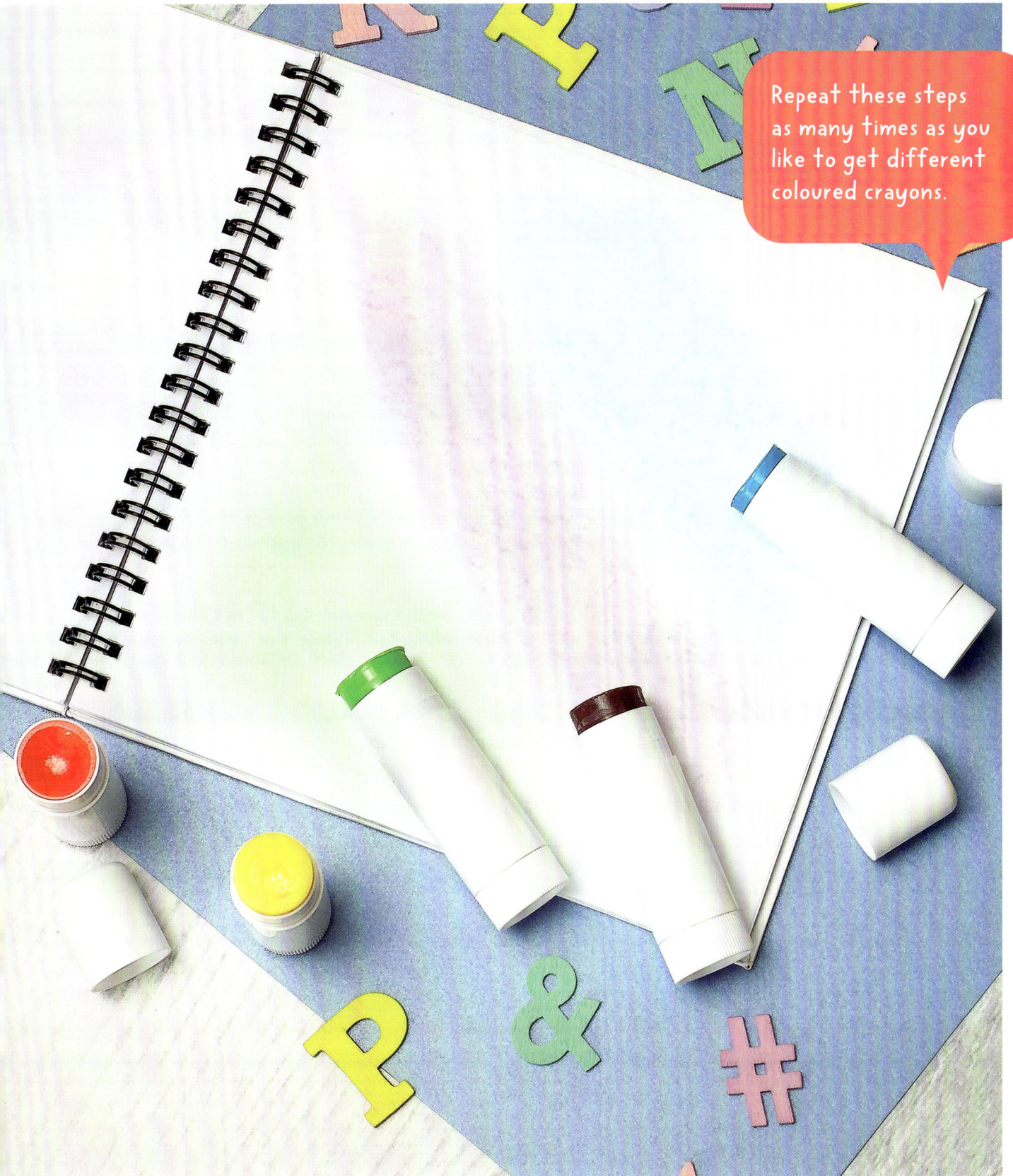

Repeat these steps as many times as you like to get different coloured crayons.

driveway clay chalk

MAKES
5

LEVEL

TIME

+ setting time

SHELF LIFE

STORE

WHAT YOU NEED

60 g white clay

50 g arrowroot flour

50 g water

colouring
x5; see pages 14-16

TOOLS

medium mixing bowl

scales

mixing spoon

small mixing bowls
x5

plate
lined with baking paper

container
lid optional

LET'S GET MAKING

1. Grab the medium mixing bowl and weigh in the white clay, arrowroot flour and water.

2. Mix really well, until the mixture is smooth, and there are no lumps left – it is very thick so you'll need to use your muscles!

3. Divide the mixture evenly between the small mixing bowls and add a different colouring to each one, then mix well.

4. Starting with one colour, scoop up the mixture into your hands, it might help to wet them just a little, and roll it into a log (not too thin!).

5. Place it onto the plate and then repeat with each batch of mixture.

6. Leave your chalk to set at room temperature – this may take a few days, then pop them in the container.

TIME TO PLAY

Find a driveway, concrete footpath or chalkboard and draw away.

Your drawings should wash away easily with water.

treasure egg

WHAT YOU NEED

35 g liquid castile soap

25 g dirt
remove any lumps

25 g sand

20 g fine salt

10 g white clay

10 g plain flour

small treasure
figurine, toy dinosaur,
fairy, mini eraser, shell etc.

TOOLS

small mixing bowl

scales

mixing spoon

small dish

container
lid optional

LET'S GET MAKING

1. Grab the mixing bowl and weigh in all of the ingredients (except the treasure!). Mix well.

2. Grab half of the mixture in your palm, cupping it, and patting it down a little.

3. Place your treasure in the centre and add the remaining mixture on top, so your treasure is buried within.

4. Press firmly, pat and mould the mixture to look like an egg shape (sometimes it may help to wet your hands a little).

5. Set your treasure egg aside to dry on the small dish – this will take 3-4 days, then pop it in the container.

TIME TO PLAY

Use something like a stick, wooden skewer or toothpick to gently chip away at the dirt until you discover the treasure inside.

LEVEL

TIME

+ drying time

SHELF LIFE

STORE

'I want these at my next birthday party!'

The longer you leave your egg to dry the better it will be, so if your egg feels soft, or breaks apart too easily, it may need more drying time.

fossil excavation

WHAT YOU NEED

50 g arrowroot flour

50 g white clay

50 g water

fossil-like object

TOOLS

small mixing bowl

scales

mixing spoon

mould
200 g capacity; shallow

container
lid optional

LET'S GET MAKING

1. Grab the mixing bowl and weigh in the arrowroot flour, white clay and water. Mix well (it will feel thick and sticky).

2. Scoop half of the mixture into the mould and spread it evenly to cover the bottom.

3. Place the fossil in the centre and press down gently.

4. Pop the rest of the mixture into the mould and cover the fossil. Smooth the top (it helps to have wet fingers for this).

5. Set it aside to dry – this will take 3-4 days at least, then pop it in the container.

TIME TO PLAY

Use something like a stick, wooden skewer or toothpick to gently chip away until you reveal the fossil inside. See if you can chisel in a way where you can see the fossil imprint on the 'cement'.

You can leave it in the mould or take it out – it's up to you.

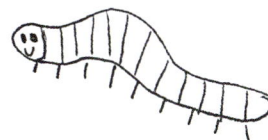

LEVEL

TIME

+ drying time

SHELF LIFE

STORE

stretchy spotty sticky goop

MAKES
130 g

LEVEL

TIME

SHELF LIFE

STORE

WHAT YOU NEED

60 g water

10 g chia seeds

colouring
optional; must be liquid;
see pages 14-16

5 drops of essential oils
optional; see page 13

1/2 tsp olive oil

60 g arrowroot flour

TOOLS

medium mixing bowl

scales

whisk

measuring spoon

mixing spoon

container with lid

LET'S GET MAKING

1. Grab the mixing bowl and weigh in the water and chia seeds.

2. Add the colouring and essential oils (if you're using them) and whisk well.

3. Let it rest for 30 minutes (the mixture will become thick and gloopy).

4. Measure in the olive oil and whisk again.

5. Now weigh in the arrowroot flour and stir until it feels too thick to use a spoon.

6. Knead the mixture with your hands until it is really smooth and stretchy, then transfer your goop into the container.

TIME TO PLAY

Play with this goop with clean hands, on a clean surface, and be prepared for messy, sticky fun!

The goop will become less sticky (and less stretchy) as the hours roll on. Wet your hands to get it back to its maximum stickiness!

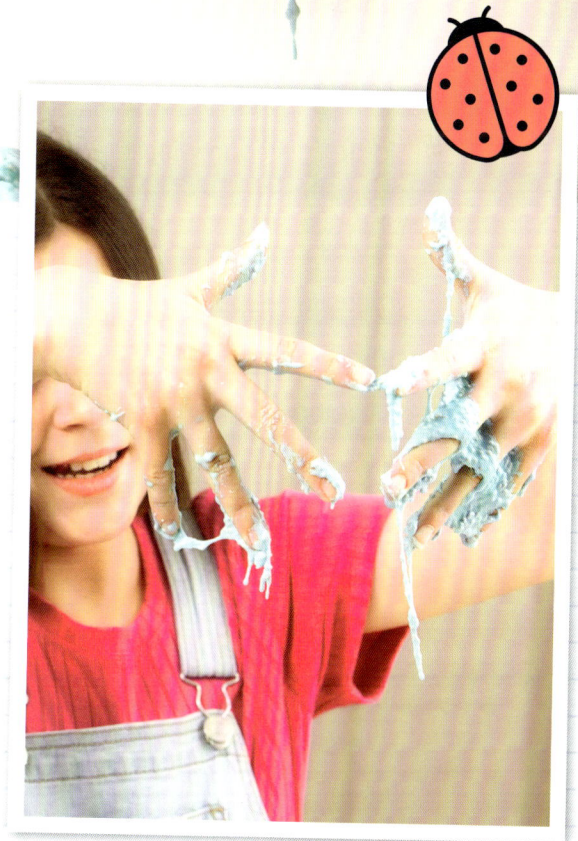

rubber flubber

LEVEL

TIME

+ cooling time

SHELF LIFE

STORE

WHAT YOU NEED

250 g water

1 tbsp psyllium husk
make sure it's super fine

1/4 tsp agar agar powder

colouring
optional; see pages 14-16

5 drops of essential oils
optional; see page 13

TOOLS

large saucepan with lid
4 L capacity

scales

measuring spoon(s)

mixing spoon

stovetop

timer

spatula

plate
large; dinner-size

container with lid

LET'S GET MAKING

1. Grab the saucepan and weigh in the water, and measure in the psyllium husk and agar agar powder.

2. Add the colouring and essential oils (if you're using them), and mix well.

3. Place the saucepan on the stovetop (no lid), on high heat and watch for the first bubble.

4. As soon as you see the first bubble, reduce the heat to moderate-high, pop the lid on and wait for exactly 3 minutes (use a timer). Do not stir.

5. Switch the heat off and use the spatula to transfer the mixture onto the plate to cool.

   ★ Careful - HOT!

6. Once the mixture has cooled down a little, it is ready to play with (it is most fun while it is warm!).

7. Keep your flubber in the container when you're not playing.

TIME TO PLAY

Play with your flubber on a clean surface, with clean hands.

Keep watching the stovetop - if it looks like it might boil over, lift the lid briefly.

Once your flubber starts breaking apart and you no longer find it fun and flubbery, you can bring it back to life by doing the following:

1. Pop your Rubber Flubber back into the saucepan and spread it out to cover the bottom.

2. Measure in 2 tablespoons of water.

3. Place the saucepan on the stovetop (no lid), on moderate-high heat and watch for the first bubble.

4. Let the mixture heat for 2-3 minutes or until you see it starting to reform. Do not stir.

5. Switch off the heat and use the spatula to transfer the mixture onto the plate to cool.

6. This can be repeated a few times with the same batch of flubber.

If the mixture sticks to the bottom of the saucepan, just fill it with a little water and leave it for a while - it'll soften and be easy to peel off.

'The making and mixing of the stuff together. The texture and feeling of the goodies are always cool.

JESSE (11)

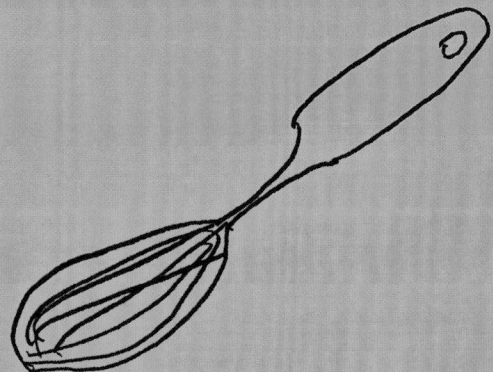

fun dough

MAKES 355 g

WHAT YOU NEED

100 g hot water

35 g fine salt

15 g citric acid

110 g arrowroot flour

70 g plain flour
plus extra to dust
your work surface

25 g olive oil

colouring
see pages 14-16

5 drops of essential oils
optional; see page 13

TOOLS

kettle

medium mixing bowl

scales

mixing spoon

container with lid

Check out the Soapy
Dough on page 67 for a
gluten-free alternative.

LET'S GET MAKING

1. Boil the kettle (make sure there is enough water inside).

2. Grab the mixing bowl and weigh in the hot water, salt and citric acid, and stir well.

3. Now weigh in the arrowroot flour, plain flour and olive oil, and add the colouring, and essential oils (if you're using them).

4. Mix until the dough starts forming.

5. Dust your work surface with a little extra flour and pop the dough on top.

6. Knead until it is soft and stretchy, then transfer your dough into the container.

TIME TO PLAY

Play, knead, pretend cook, make people and flowers and trees – your imagination has no limits!

'This is like the best dough I've ever felt.'

⚡ Double or triple this recipe for more colours.

LEVEL

TIME

SHELF LIFE

STORE

cocoa shaping sand

MAKES 215 g

WHAT YOU NEED

140 g arrowroot flour

55 g olive oil

20 g cocoa powder

TOOLS

medium mixing bowl

scales

mixing spoon

container with lid

LET'S GET MAKING

1. Grab the mixing bowl and weigh in all of the ingredients. Give it a little mix.

2. Then, get your hands in there and rub the ingredients together between your fingers.

3. Your sand is ready when it holds its shape when squeezed, but breaks apart easily.

4. Transfer your shaping sand into the container.

TIME TO PLAY

Make shapes and smash them down; it's fun and smells great!

LEVEL

TIME

SHELF LIFE

STORE

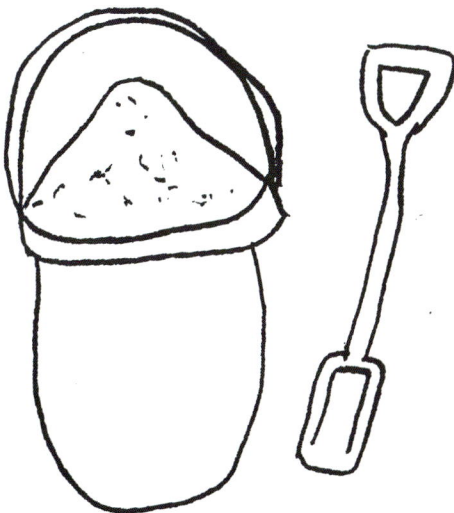

sand-not-sand

MAKES
250 g

WHAT YOU NEED

100 g rice
brown or white

100 g plain flour

20 g water

2 tsp turmeric powder

25 g olive oil

TOOLS

oven

blender

scales

medium mixing bowl

measuring spoon

mixing spoon

baking tray

timer

oven mitt or tea towel

container with lid

LET'S GET MAKING

1. Preheat the oven to 180 °C (or 160 °C fan-forced).

2. Grab the blender jug and weigh in the white rice, then blend until it is fine (like powder). Empty it into the mixing bowl.

3. Now weigh in the plain flour and water, and measure in the turmeric powder. Mix, mix, mix.

4. Transfer the mixture onto the baking tray, and break apart any little clumps with your fingers.

5. Place it in the oven for 15 minutes, mixing midway. Use a timer.

   ★ Use the oven mitt or tea towel.

6. Turn the oven off and remove the baking tray.

7. Once the mixture has cooled a little (give it 5 minutes or so), transfer it back into the mixing bowl, and weigh in the olive oil. Mix well.

8. Transfer your sand into the container.

TIME TO PLAY

Drive your toy cars or diggers through this sand, maybe add some building blocks and create a worksite. The possibilities are endless!

You might find it easier to use your hands.

LEVEL

TIME

SHELF LIFE

STORE

melting putty

MAKES 260 g

LEVEL

TIME

SHELF LIFE

STORE

WHAT YOU NEED

140 g arrowroot flour

100 g aloe vera gel
not the fresh garden variety

20 g olive oil

colouring
optional; see pages 14-16

TOOLS

medium mixing bowl

scales

mixing spoon

container with lid

LET'S GET MAKING

1. Grab the mixing bowl and weigh in the arrowroot flour, aloe vera gel and olive oil.

2. Add the colouring (if you're using it) and mix until the ingredients start coming together.

3. Then, transfer the mixture onto a clean work surface and knead for a minute or so. Your putty is ready when it can be made into a smooth ball, and then starts melting in your hands.

   ✳ *If you find your putty 'melts' too quickly, just knead in a little extra flour.*

4. Pop your putty into the container.

TIME TO PLAY

Build a shape and watch how fast (or slow) it melts. Why not race your friends and see whose can live the longest!

foaming sludge

LEVEL

TIME

SHELF LIFE

WHAT YOU NEED

70 g bicarb soda

25 g arrowroot flour

15 g citric acid

colouring
optional; must be powder;
see pages 14-16

25 g water

TOOLS

small mixing bowl

scales

mixing spoon

LET'S GET MAKING

1. Grab the mixing bowl and weigh in the bicarb soda, arrowroot flour and citric acid.

2. Add the colouring (if you're using it) and mix well.

3. Now weigh in the water, then mix and watch!

TIME TO PLAY

Your sludge has a lifespan of about 10 minutes. Sprinkle it, scoop it up, flatten it down, watch it foam and grow on your playing surface.

Sometimes bicarb soda can be irritating to your skin so you might want to use a spoon or pop on some gloves.

If you keep playing with your sludge, you'll notice that after a while, it will turn into something a little different in texture – but just as fun!

salt dough shapes

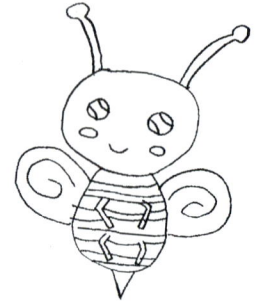

MAKES 8-10

LEVEL

TIME

+ drying time

SHELF LIFE

WHAT YOU NEED

65 g fine salt

65 g plain flour
plus extra to dust your work surface

50 g water

TOOLS

medium mixing bowl

scales

mixing spoon

rolling pin

cookie cutters

baking tray
lined with baking paper

metal straw

Why not use the Paper Paint from page 81.

LET'S GET MAKING

1. Grab the mixing bowl and weigh in all of the ingredients, and mix until the dough starts forming.

2. Dust your work surface with a little extra flour and pop the dough on top. Knead until it is smooth and well formed.

3. Now use the rolling pin to roll out the dough until it is about 0.5 cm thick.

4. Use the cookie cutters to create as many shapes as you can fit and carefully place them onto the baking tray.

5. Use the straw to punch a hole in your shapes, about 0.5 cm from the edge (so that you can hang them later).

6. Roll the dough scraps together into a ball and repeat steps 3-5 until you have no more dough left.

7. Leave your shapes in the sun for a few days to harden up, flipping them occasionally, before painting and hanging.

TIME TO PLAY

Hang them up or use them as gift tags – or come up with your own ideas!

You could also dry these in a very low oven (about 100 °C). If your shapes start to puff up in the oven, pop a sheet of baking paper and a second baking tray on top to keep them flattened.

114

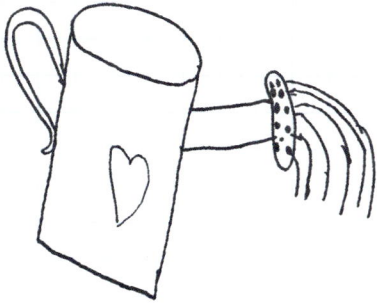

garden stew

This is a very special recipe for a magical Garden Stew. If you follow the instructions and make a wish, it might even come true!

Firstly, grab the following garden items and pop them into a bucket or bowl:

5-10 small twigs

5-10 flowers

5-10 leaves

1 handful of fresh grass

1 cup of dirt or sand

Now sprinkle over **1/2 cup of bicarb soda** and mix well.

Slowly pour **1 cup of vinegar** into your Garden Stew and watch it sizzle, bubble and burst. It is during this bit that I recommend casting a positive, happy spell.

Another idea for a Garden Stew is to set a challenge for your family and friends, and get them to collect 3 things that are brown, blue, green, white, yellow and pink, before adding the bicarb soda and vinegar.

leafetti confetti

Traditional confetti uses precious resources, and is sometimes made from materials that aren't kind to the environment. Why not make your own natural version? Simply collect a whole stack of **leaves** from the garden or park, grab a **hole punch** and start punching!

When you have heaps, you could throw it around the garden, or you can dry them out and store them if you like. Another idea is to stick your Leafetti Confetti on paper and create a work of art. You might even like to add rose petals and lavender buds to your Leafetti Confetti.

frozen fun

Grab an **ice cube tray** (the bigger the better) and pop an object or two inside each compartment. Things like **flowers, seeds, leaves, stones, rice, erasers, shells, small toys** and **figurines** work well. Top each space with water (you could even colour it!) and carefully transfer the tray into the freezer.

Once they're frozen, it's time to have fun! Why not see how long the ice cubes take to melt on different surfaces like your driveway, mailbox, grass, a piece of foil in the sun, or drop a few in the bath with you? You could even sprinkle salt on top, or fill a bowl with very warm water and then use a syringe to suck up and squirt over the ice to melt it away and reveal your little treasures!

afterword

If I can leave you with one final thought, it is this ...

Be curious, beautiful children. Ask questions, make better choices for yourself and for our divine planet. Then, tell somebody – tell everybody – just how awesome a natural life is.

It is my hope that making natural DIY spotty goop becomes as common as making cookies. Can you help with that? Yes, yes you can!

WHERE TO FIND ME

- facebook.com/theinspiredlittlepot
- instagram.com/theinspiredlittlepot
- pinterest.com.au/theinspiredlittlepot
- youtube.com/theinspiredlittlepot
- linkedin.com/in/krissy-ballinger
- theinspiredlittlepot.com.au
- hello@theinspiredlittlepot.com.au

acknowledgements

The bulk of this book was written and perfected during early 2020, when we all learned how to slow down, as a nasty little bug made its way around the globe.

While the impact was huge on so many lives, I chose to see the silver linings, and goodness me, they were everywhere: generally, people were spending more time with those they loved most, spending less money, completing home projects, travelling less, walking more, cooking from scratch … Canals, rivers and lakes began to clear up, smog and pollution was lifting, mountains came out of hiding, dolphins, turtles and sea life came out to play. Many of us paused to consider how we've been treating the planet, and many of us have pledged to do better in the future.

So, as I wrote this book, I spent a lot of time reflecting with a little buzz in my tummy, knowing that it would be appreciated now, more than ever.

There are literally hundreds, if not thousands, of people I could thank right now. And I don't use the word 'thanks' lightly, either. This is the goosebumpy kind of gratitude.

My beautiful family – you are amazeballs; I love you more than unicorns and rainbows, and I'm beyond excited that you're mine to keep.

My amazing friends, who may as well be family – your support, encouragement, patience and help is something I am so so so grateful for. I'm privileged to have your friendship.

The humans who helped me with idea-bouncing, reading, proofing, editing, designing, photographing, scouting, testing – your talent, skill, interest and commitment is actually priceless. I am so lucky to have found you all; you're the perfect pieces of my book-writing puzzle.

The Inspired Little Pot community – I wouldn't be where I am today if it wasn't for your support, respect and encouragement. I've learned a lot from you, and not a day goes by that I'm not grateful to have a community that is willing to learn from me too.

Last, but absolutely not least, to the little humans who were a very, very important part of the making of this book – you are all rock stars! From testing and playing with my recipes, to the totally amazing drawings you did for me, plus the photo shoots; it was an absolute honour to have your help and this book would not have been complete without it.

You, beautiful children, are the leaders of the future. What you do today matters, so be curious, never stop asking questions and make decisions with thought and compassion.

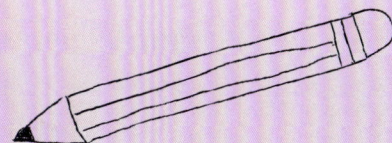

measurement conversion chart

grams	ounces
5	0.2
10	0.4
15	0.5
20	0.7
25	0.9
30	1.1
35	1.2
40	1.4
45	1.6
50	1.8
55	1.9
60	2.1
65	2.3
70	2.5
80	2.8
90	3.2
100	3.5
110	3.9
130	4.6
140	4.9
150	5.3
180	6.3
200	7.1
230	8.1
250	8.8
300	10.6
355	12.5

centimetres	inches
0.5	0.2
2	0.8
3	1.2
5	2.0
6	2.4
15	5.9

celsius	fahrenheit
60	140
70	158
100	212
160	320
180	356
200	392

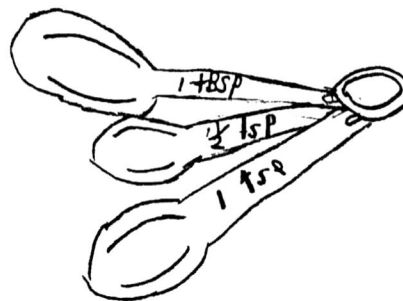

'You can make things whenever you want and it's better for your body.'

LUCAS (8)

index

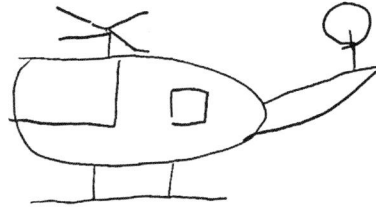

Copyright

NATIONAL LIBRARY OF AUSTRALIA

A catalogue record for this work is available from the National Library of Australia